Table of Contents

Acknowledgements

Although I began making "Layered Waves" in 1998, making waves to wear was new territory for me. I would not have been able to write this book without the creative energy I received from family, friends, students, quilt shop owners and quilt guilds. All of you have supported and encouraged me to keep moving forward in this new territory. A special thank you to:

Trish Palmer, the special friend who encouraged me in 2008 to make that first jacket and also suggested the need for a doll jacket. You are so smart Trish!

Marilyn Nelson (Bluebird Quilt Studios, Nampa, Idaho) who has been teaching jacket workshops from my *Layered Waves* book for quite some time. Your enthusiasm, experience and helpful insights were indispensable!

Cat Allard (ZenCatArt) for your constant friendship, support and tailoring lessons - over a cup of tea in your kitchen, in my studio and via Skype! It was such a comfort to know that you were only a tap on the keyboard away and always ready for a mini-fashion show and consultation. You're the best!

Sandra Kunz, for modeling "Energetic."
Red has always been *your* color!

Lisa Cruse (Ambrosia Cottage) for patiently leading me through basic clothing techniques over coffee in town and in my studio. Thanks for taking the photo of me in the "Playful" jacket and for modeling the "Wild Woman" jacket with your new hat pattern.
Your creative energy is contagious!

Hoffman California Fabrics for providing some of the beautiful Bali Batiks. The fabrics make the jackets!

Juli Eckmeier Cosack for suggesting the idea of the shrug and modeling the "Frisky" bolero shrug with Griffin. You are both so adorable!

Walter Eckmeier, my creative husband and best friend, who supports me with every endeavor I undertake. Thank you for all of your hard work with this book design, photography and layout.
Are you ready for the next book?

My Top Secret Jacket Retreat Team
What a great team! We enjoyed a wonderful weekend together at Wisdom House creating Wearable Waves. We laughed and learned a lot! Your positive energy and helpful suggestions were perfect.

Here they are modeling their jackets in various stages of completeion:

Donna Nicklis, Susan Kozikowski, Katie Greenwood, Kathie Stein and Terry Greenstein
(back row left to right)

Angie DeLuca, Ginny Dodd, Jacqueline Fleishman and Carol Robinson
(middle row left to far right)

Thomasina Levy, Rosemary Dziubinski and Maddie Burke *(front row left to right)*

Introduction

Here is an "offspring" of my *Layered Waves* book, which uses my layered topstitching technique to create a textured fabric with wild curves and angles. At the request of friends and students, I am expanding on the "Flowing Wearables" chapter found on pages 82 - 85 of *Layered Waves*.

Follow the instructions in this book to use a **lightweight sweatshirt** for your pattern pieces OR use a **favorite pattern** combined with a lightweight polyester fleece. The sweatshirt material and the fleece provide a wonderful base for quilting and double as an easy inner lining.

There are **ten casual open front jacket styles**, from which you can choose. Each one showcases flowing lines that are designed to flatter your figure. Use the line drawings in each chapter to help you envision the jacket in different color combinations or with different sleeve styles. You have my permission to copy those pages for your personal use.

Variations include a **vest** and a **bolero shrug with three-quarter sleeves**. The last chapter includes the patterns to make a **teddy bear vest** and an **18" doll jacket**. Simply irresistible!

Before you begin your project, please read through "The Essentials" chapter carefully.

Have fun makin' waves to wear!

Karen

About Karen

Karen coming out of her shell to create waves to wear.

Karen Eckmeier, aka The Quilted Lizard, is an award-winning fiber artist, international teacher, author, and pattern designer. With a background in drawing, but no sewing experience Karen taught herself how to sew in order to make her first quilt. That was back in 1987 and she's been hooked on fabric ever since.

Her books *Happy Villages, Accidental Landscapes, Layered Waves* and *Wearable Waves* emphasize her no-stress approach to playing with fabric, whether it be raw-edge collage or her layered topstitching technique, Karen believes that lots of intense playing tends to yield wonderful results, and she shares this philosophy in her workshops, books, and patterns. Students always go home with an "I can do that!" attitude.

The Essentials

Select 6 Fabrics

Color, Scale and Value

Wearable Waves jackets are based on six fabrics. Choose a color palette that you LOVE to wear, either one color or a combination of colors. Then look for a variety of fabric prints in a range of values (light, medium and dark) that contrast with each other.

Here are examples of six fabrics that work well together. There is a **variety in the scale of the prints** and there is **contrast in value** so that the fabrics do not blend into each other.

Two Colors

Large scale leaf print (length of the branch motif is 4") + small scale line print + medium scale circle/dot print + medium scale crackle print + two solid-like blues.

One Color Gradation + Accent Color

Large scale floral (width of largest flower is 5") + two solid-like pinks + medium scale floral print + small scale print + accent color of a dark brown.

Use this formula to select a variety of fabric prints that create a balanced design.

- 2 small scale prints
- 1 medium scale print
- 1 "large" scale print (not huge, but larger than the other prints)
- 2 solids or solid-like (can be a subtle low contrast print)

> **Hint:**
> *When working in a two color palette, look for fabrics that incorporate both colors in the design.*

Multi-Color Print + Coordinating Fabrics

Multi-color stripe (second from top) and prints in a range of contrasting values, colors and prints.

Two Colors

Large scale gingko leaf print (largest leaf motif is 2½" wide) + solid black + solid-like red + medium scale paisley + two small prints.

The medium and dark values work well together due to the high contrast between the prints.

What Is Value?

Value is the relative lightness or darkness of a color. Different colors can have the same value. For example: Squint your eyes as you look at the fabrics below on the left.

different colors 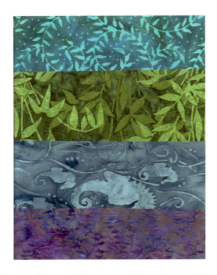  same value

The edges of the fabrics blend into each other. If you have trouble seeing how the edges of the fabrics meld, look at the black and white version on the right. Once the color is gone, it's much easier to see that these fabrics blend together and therefore are the same value.

How can you see *your* fabrics in black and white? **At home:** Scan the fabrics or take a digital photo. Then edit the image on the computer screen to black and white. Another option is to use a copy machine to make a black and white copy of the fabrics. **In a workshop setting:** use the black & white setting on your digital camera to view your fabrics in black & white on the LCD screen. Most digital point and shoot cameras have this feature.

Look at the two photos below. Notice how much easier it is to see the dark, medium and light values in the black and white version on the right.

dark values

different colors

medium values

light values

A value finder is another great tool for seeing values. Simply look at the fabrics through a red or green piece of plastic (or cellophane) and the colors disappear. Red value finders work best with warm colors (except red) and green value finders work best with cool colors (except green). When in doubt use both colors.

Design Hints

Keep these fashion tips in mind as you select fabrics for your jacket.

✳ **Are you smiling?**
Hold the six fabrics up to your face in a mirror or drape them over your shoulder. How do the colors make you feel? The answer should be an immediate GREAT! If not, keep looking.

✳ **Colored Pencils**
Make copies of the line drawings. Fill in the designs with colored pencils to help you envision the jacket or vest in your chosen fabrics and/or a different color palette.

✳ **Dark Colors**
... are "slimming."

✳ **Light Colors**
... add visual weight. Use them sparingly in your jacket.

✳ **Large Scale Prints**
... can make your body look larger and can be unflattering if placed in the wrong section of the jacket. Be careful not to place large floral motifs or circles in the chest area!

✳ **Vertical Lines**
... in a fabric pattern design are more flattering than horizontal lines. They also make you look taller.

✳ **Go for Contrast**
Think about what color top/blouse/shirt you will wear underneath the jacket. This will help you decide which colors to use on either side of the front panels.

✳ **Look in the mirror often**
... as you create the Layered Waves fabric for each pattern piece. Hold the fabric up to yourself where it will be placed in the jacket. Look carefully at the placement of the fabric prints, colors and design shapes on your body. This will help you decide if any changes need to be made with the placement of certain prints, colors or shapes. For example: If a large circle motif appears in your chest area, now is the time to replace that fabric, or use less of that fabric in that area.

Yardage Chart

The predominant color or fabric in the jacket is referred to as the "Primary Color/Fabric" in the chart below. This should be your favorite color or fabric in your selection of six fabrics. You will need the most yardage of this fabric.

The yardage chart gives a guideline to the minimum and maximum amount of yardage needed to create a Wearable Waves jacket. If, like me, you change your mind during the process of making the jacket or you fear running out of a particular fabric, then I would suggest buying the yardage in the "Maximum Yardage" column.

For the vest and shrug variations, refer to the "Minimum Yardage" column.

Bindings on Wearable Waves jackets are made using the scraps from the original six fabrics. For a binding in a fabric other than one of your six fabrics, figure on an additional ½ yard.

ADULT	MINIMUM YARDAGE*	MAXIMUM YARDAGE*
S-M	½ yard each of 5 fabrics and 1 yard of the Primary Color/Fabric	1 yard each of 6 fabrics (+ extra Primary Color/Fabric)
L-XL	¾ yard each of 5 fabrics and 1¼ yard of the Primary Color/Fabric	1¼ yard each of 6 fabrics (+ extra Primary Color/Fabric)
2XL-3XL	1¼ yard each of 5 fabrics and 1½ yards of the Primary Color/Fabric	1½ yards each of 6 fabrics (+ extra Primary Color/Fabric)

*Directional fabrics (stripes or designs with an up/down orientation) require twice as much yardage or need to be pieced to get the desired length.

Supplies

- Crewneck sweatshirt for pattern pieces **OR** your favorite jacket/vest pattern + fleece
- 6 coordinated fabrics – 100% cottons
- Sewing machine with the following presser feet:
    - Straight stitching foot
    - Zigzag foot
    - Walking foot is a MUST
    - Free motion quilting foot (optional)
    - ¼" seam foot
- Serger (optional – zigzag stitch works fine to finish edges)
- Cotton or polyester threads
- Iron and ironing board

- Large and small scissors
- Rotary cutter and long ruler
- Small and large rotary cutting mats
- Tape measure
- Basting thread and needle (or safety pins for basting)
- Fabric marking pencil and/or marker
- Long pins and pin cushion/holder
- Seam ripper
- Sharp #10 needle (or your choice of a hand sewing needle)
- Buttons – optional

Buying the Sweatshirt

Directions in the book use a sweatshirt base, however, **all of the designs can be adapted to fit your favorite jacket or vest pattern**. Polyester fleece works well as a substitute for sweatshirt material.

Why use a sweatshirt?
- *It already fits*
- *Only basic sewing skills are required*
- *Easy lining – the smooth side of the sweatshirt becomes the lining*
- *Quilts* beautifully. The sweatshirt serves as both the batting and the bottom fabric layer. It provides just the right amount of loft to show off the quilting stitches*

* I am stretching the term "quilt," since we only have two layers in these quilted jackets: The Layered Waves fabric + the sweatshirt base. By definition a quilt consists of three layers: Bottom fabric, batting and a top fabric. It is the quilting stitch that holds all three layers together.

Weight & Style

Look for a basic adult unisex crew neck sweatshirt in a **lightweight** cotton/polyester blend weighing **between 7oz. - 8oz**.

Sleeves need to be set-in (not raglan) with **seams ideally at the shoulder or slightly off the shoulder** by not more than 2". Most crew neck sweatshirts have slightly off the shoulder seams, which will work fine with the designs in the book.

Color

Select a sweatshirt that matches the color palette of your fabrics. A great source for low cost sweatshirts is online at **www.Jiffyshirts.com**. This company offers a **wide selection of colors** and brands at a **reasonable cost** with speedy delivery.

Another option is to use an old sweatshirt, because you already know it fits! If the sweatshirt has a fun logo, you may consider letting the logo show on the inside as an unexpected fashion statement.

Size

Sweatshirts are made for a man's broad shoulders and narrow hips. This makes it tricky to find the right size sweatshirt for a woman's curves.

Use the chart below to help you decide which size is right for you. It is critical to **start with the correct size sweatshirt**, not too small and not too big, otherwise you will need the knowledge of a seamstress friend to tailor your jacket to fit your body.

My goal is to keep the jacket construction at a beginner sewing level. Simple fitting adjustments are made after the jacket pattern pieces have been quilted and the assembly has begun.

Sweatshirt Size Suggestions

Slender sizes S and M - buy the size that you normally wear

Well-endowed sizes L and XL - buy one size larger

Curvaceous sizes 2XL and 3XL - buy two sizes larger

ADULT	Body Width (across front)	Body Length (not including 2.5" bottom band)	Shoulder Seam	Sleeve Length (includes 2.5" cuff band)	Sleeve Width (opened flat)
S (34-36)	20"	23"	5" - 7"	21" - 22"	21" - 23"
M (38-40)	22"	24"	6" - 8"	21" - 22"	21" - 23"
L (42-44)	24"	25"	7" - 9"	21" - 22"	21" - 23"
XL (46-48)	26"	26"	8" - 11"	22" - 24"	25" - 27"
2XL (50-52)	28"	27"	9" - 12"	23" - 26"	26" - 28"
3XL (54-56)	30"	28"	9" - 12"	23" - 26"	26" - 28"

The numbers in this chart combine a range of measurements taken from 5 different brands of crew neck sweatshirts.

Here's How to Get Started

➤ Choose a Wearable Waves style: jacket, vest or shrug and go to that chapter

➤ Select colors and fabrics according to the chapter guidelines

➤ Refer to the "Layered Waves in 6 Easy Steps" instructions to create the fabrics for each of the pattern pieces as suggested in each chapter

Cutting the Sweatshirt

Machine-wash the sweatshirt and the six fabrics in cold water and dry on low heat in the dryer. Some brands of "pre-shrunk" sweatshirts can shrink up to an inch in overall length and sleeve length and others will stay true to their original shape. It's best to find out now.

Try the sweatshirt on to determine if the cuff bands are needed for sleeve length. Cuff bands may be left on if needed, however, the bottom band and collar band are always removed for a Wearable Waves jacket.

If you are making the **bolero shrug** *("Frisky" page 60), the* **vest** *("Cheerful" page 66), the* **doll jacket** *or the* **teddy bear vest** *("Irresistibles" pages 72-79) please go directly to that chapter to begin specific cutting instructions.*

1. Use scissors to carefully cut off the bottom band and cuff bands right next to the seam lines.

   How long do you want your jacket to be? Do you want it to cover your hips or do you want it to extend to mid hips or nestle at your waist? Mark this line and use a rotary cutter and ruler to cut about 1" longer than you need. Sleeve length can be adjusted later.

2. Lay the sweatshirt flat (smooth side out) on a table. Fold and crease the sides so that they align exactly with the underarm seam. If the sweatshirt has side seams, remove them with a seam ripper.

   Use scissors to cut up the sides and stop exactly where the armhole seam intersects with the sleeve seam. It is important that the side seam flows continuously right into the sleeve seam. Repeat for the other side.

3. With a seam ripper undo both sleeve seams, NOT the armhole seams. Pull out all loose threads. If the cuff bands are going to remain on the sleeves, carefully remove the seam to open up the cuff band. Use an iron to steam press the cuffs flat. Press the cuff seam towards the sleeve.

> **Seam Ripper or Scissors?**
> *To keep the original fit of the jacket, it is worth the effort to carefully open seams with a seam ripper.*

For the "Playful" and "Wild Woman" one-piece constructions jackets, skip to step #5.

4. Open up both sleeves and lay them flat with the smooth side of the sweatshirt facing up. Make a registration mark with a fabric marker on the sleeve, where the shoulder seam connects with the center of the sleeve. Label this registration mark with a line and "R" for the right sleeve and "L" for the left sleeve.

Use a **contrasting fabric marker to mark registration lines** approximately every 2" on armholes/sleeves – **not tailor's chalk** (it wears away) on the **smooth side of sweatshirt.** For a dark sweatshirt use a metallic marker.

Add some **creative symbols (triangles, circles, squares) to the registration lines** so they don't all look the same (see photo). This is extremely helpful when setting the sleeves back into the armholes, especially if one of the sleeves has changed slightly in size due to quilting. The extra little symbols make it obvious, as to which registration lines go together. If you use different registration lines on both sleeves, this will also prevent you from inserting the wrong sleeve into the wrong armhole. The sweatshirt sleeve pattern pieces are not always exactly the same size!

> **Left or Right?**
> *Remember that the smooth side will become the INSIDE of the jacket, so mark your right and left sleeves carefully, it is very easy to confuse them! Try it on if necessary to be sure which is the right and left sleeve. Label the front and back of the sleeves on the smooth side for easy reference.*

5. Carefully undo both armhole seams with a seam ripper.

6. If the sweatshirt has a label, remove it and mark the back of the sweatshirt, on the fuzzy side, so that you don't confuse it with the front pattern piece.

7. Carefully undo the shoulder seams and collar band seam with a seam ripper. Pull out the threads.

   Stop here if you are making the **"Natural" Jacket,** *which keeps the front pattern piece un-cut until after the Layered Waves are added.*

8. For all other jacket styles, fold the front piece of the sweatshirt in half. Mark this centerline and cut with scissors or a rotary cutter. You now have 5 jacket pattern pieces: 2 fronts, 1 back and 2 sleeves.

   Continue on the next page for the **"Playful" and "Wild Woman"** *one-piece construction jackets.*

   For the **bolero shrug** *go to page 63 to continue cutting instructions for the front pattern pieces.*

"Playful" and "Wild Woman" one-piece construction jackets (pages 50-59)

For the waves to flow smoothly over the shoulder in the "Playful" and "Wild Woman" jackets, the double needle cover-stitching needs to be removed from the shoulder and armhole seams and then basted back together.

1. Butt the edges of the shoulder seams together, so they lie flat and are NOT overlapping. Hand-baste in place with basting thread.

2. Machine stitch over the basted shoulder seams using a large zigzag stitch, in thread that matches the color of the sweatshirt. Remove the basting threads.

3. Repeat the basting and zigzag stitching to butt the right and left sleeves with the right and left armholes. You now have a jacket pattern in one-piece, which has been re-stitched flat at the shoulder and armhole seams.

   Flat is the key for one-piece construction jacket styles. The armhole/sleeve seams must be completely flat.

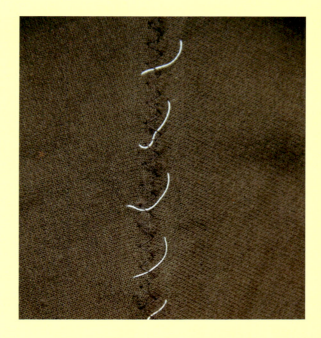

Some sweatshirt armhole/sleeves will baste back together flat without any adjustments, while other sweatshirt sleeves will need to be trimmed to create a flat seam.

To make this seam flat, place the curved edge of the armhole on top of the sleeve so they overlap.

Use the curved edge of the armhole as a guide to cut a matching curve on the sleeve (the new curved line to be cut is marked on the sleeve with dotted chalk lines in the photo).

Baste the armholes and sleeves together as directed in steps #1 and #2 for the shoulder seams.

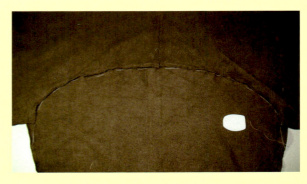

Optional cutting adjustments to make armhole/sleeve seams lie flat

Layered Waves in 6 Easy Steps

Layered Waves is my layered topstitching technique that uses free-form rotary cutting to cut wild curves and dramatic angles to create a fabric that has a wonderful texture. There is not a right or wrong way to cut Layered Waves, just your way.

Begin with a fabric strip approximately 3″ wide x the length of the edge of the pattern piece + 2″

Always start at the edge of the pattern piece and work across to the other side of the pattern piece, unless the specific jacket directions instruct otherwise.

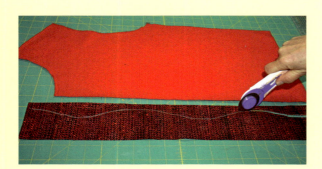

1. **Cut a gentle curve** on one edge of the 3″ strip with the rotary cutter. Practice the cutting motion a few times with the blade closed until you get used to the idea of cutting a free-form curve. You can also draw a curve with chalk if that makes you more comfortable. Once you are ready, take a deep breath, loosen your shoulders and cut a gentle curve.

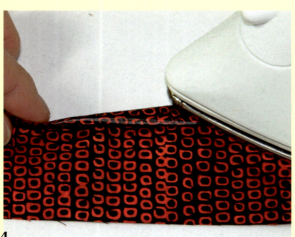

2. **Press the edge** of the curve approximately ¼″ to the wrong side of the fabric. Place the pressed curved strip on top of the next fabric in sequence. Align the straight un-pressed edge of the curved strip with the straight edge of the second fabric. **The second and subsequent fabrics do not need to be pre-cut into strips**

14

3. Cut a curve on the next fabric that is similar, but not exactly the same, to the first curve.

Vary the distance of the second curve between ½"- 3" away from the pressed curved edge. This will give the waves a sense of movement.

4. Pin with long pins every 2" perpendicular to the pressed edge.

5. Topstitch 1/8" from the pressed edge. This creates a little pleat, which is the key to the textural quality of the finished fabric.

6. Trim away: Turn the topstitched piece over and trim away the bottom fabric approximately ¼" away from the topstitched line of sewing.

Repeat these 6 steps to create a Layered Waves fabric that fits the size of the pattern piece.

> **Another Way to Begin:**
> *Cut a fabric strip approximately* **3" wide x the longest section** *of the pattern piece + 2". This approach creates some fabric waste, but eliminates the need to constantly check the size of the Layered Waves fabric to make sure it is large enough to fit the pattern piece.*

Zigzag Waves

Create dramatic points to mix in with the curves, by cutting
90° angles or greater, that match the flow of the cut curve.

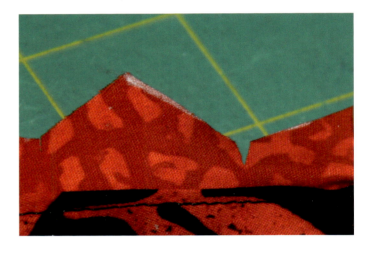

1. First cut a curve. Then draw triangles with chalk, so that the points end at the edge of the cut curve and dip down to within ½" from the topstitched line of sewing.

2. Cut along the chalk lines with scissors. Clip ¼" into the low dip between each point.

3. Press the fabric approximately ¼" to the wrong side of the fabric, overlapping at the points.

4. Place the pressed triangles on top of the next fabric in sequence. Cut the curve on the next fabric a minimum of ½" to a maximum of 3" from the top of the points.

Ribbon Waves

A ribbon wave (called a "Ripple" in the *Layered Waves* book) is a fabric wave that is overlapped by two topstitched fabrics. Each time a curve is cut in the fabric, the cut away piece has the mirror shape.

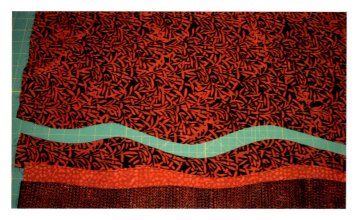

1. Press both curved edges toward the wrong side. Then place both pressed edges on top of a fabric with high contrast.

2. Slide one of the pressed curves left and right (or up and down) to create a ribbon shape.

3. Pin both pressed curved edges with the pins placed parallel to the edges. This makes topstitching much easier. Topstitch and cut away the excess fabric from the back.

Cresting Waves

A cresting wave is a fabric wave that has topstitching along both curved edges (or zigzag edges). A crest is automatically created after making a ribbon wave.

Another way to create a cresting wave is to turn the Layered Waves fabric around, so that you are working in the opposite direction. The strip that you started with is now at the top, instead of the bottom. Cut a curve on this fabric. Press the curve approximately ¼" to the wrong side of the fabric and topstitch to the next fabric in sequence to create a cresting wave.

17

Lightning Streak & Jaunty Hanging Diamond Waves

These waves are made the same way as ribbon waves, except a zig zag is cut instead of a curve. Mix in a Lightning Streak or a Jaunty Hanging Diamond Wave among the curved lines of the Layered Waves fabric for an eye catching effect.

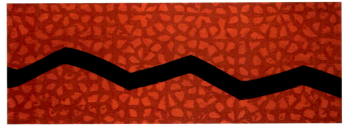

1. Begin with two 3″ strips of two contrasting fabrics that are a 4″ longer than the length of the sleeve. The extra length allows for the shifting of the strips to create the designs.

2. With scissors cut an uneven zigzag up the center of one of the fabric strips. For ease of pressing, cut the angles 90° or greater.
3. Clip ¼″ into the low dip between each point.
4. Press both zigzag cut edges approximately ¼″ toward the wrong side of the fabric. Place them on the contrasting fabric strip to create either a Lightning Streak or shift the strips to create Jaunty Hanging Diamonds waves. (see photos below)
5. Topstitch and cut away the excess fabric from the back.

Lightning Streak Wave

Jaunty Hanging Diamond Wave

Slender Points
aka Short on Fabric!!

Here's a beautiful slender point that is created when two fabrics of different lengths are used. You can plan to create these slender points or they may simply be the result of using small scraps of fabric. Whether planned or by accident, these are the steps to follow:

1. In the photo the red fabric is not the same length as the Layered Waves fabric, this creates the perfect scenario to create the Slender Point.

2. As you cut the curve on the red fabric, taper the cut to end and flow right into the previous curve.

3. Begin topstitching these two curves together 1″ in from the end of the Slender Point. This allows room for the red fabric to be pressed under later during the pressing process. (back-stitching is not needed at this step)

4. After topstitching, press the fabric so the curved edge flows smoothly from one fabric to the next. Topstitch to the next fabric in the sequence by sewing on the first fabric (see dotted chalk lines above). When you reach the previous line of stitching, overlap it with a backstitch to secure. Lift the presser foot, carry the thread over to the point marked by the chalk pencil point above. Put the presser foot down, backstitch and begin topstitching on the red fabric.

5. Clip the carrying threads on the top and underneath after the topstitching is complete. **19**

Creative Topstitching
aka Short on Fabric Too!!

It's possible that during the topstitching process, there may not be enough yardage of a particular fabric to cover a pattern piece. Don't worry! This is time to celebrate, because it is a wonderful "creative opportunity." Here's the chance to piece with topstitched curves. Topstitch two of the same fabrics together or have fun and topstitch two different fabrics together to fit the pattern piece. The exciting part is that these new topstitched lines add additional texture and become an important part of the jacket design.

Notice that the pink fabric is not large enough to cover the sweatshirt pattern piece.

Use Creative Topstitching to add another piece of fabric to make it the correct size.

Creative Topstitching makes this sleeve much more interesting.

What happens if you are ready to quilt and notice that the Layered Waves fabric has shifted and is just a bit too short to cover the sweatshirt pattern piece? A curved piece of brown fabric is "topstitched creatively" to add length and cover the pattern piece. The brown fabric is topstitched to the Layered Waves fabric, **not** to the sweatshirt pattern piece, so that the excess fabric can be trimmed from the back.

Quilting

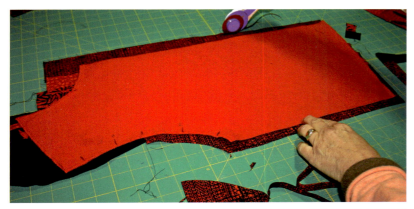

Once you have created a Layered Waves fabric to fit a pattern piece, press it well with an iron. Place the sweatshirt pattern piece (fuzzy side down) on top of the Layered Waves fabric (wrong side up). Smooth and pat the fabric and the sweatshirt pattern piece gently to remove wrinkles. Cut approximately ½"- 1" around the pattern piece edges.

Turn the unit over (unit = Layered Waves fabric + sweatshirt pattern piece), so that the Layered Waves fabric is now on top (right side up) and the pattern piece is below (fuzzy side up).

Prepare the Layered Waves for quilting by pin basting (straight pins or safety pins) or thread basting the Layered Waves fabric to the sweatshirt patterns pieces.

All of the quilting on Wearable Waves jackets can be done with the **walking foot or even feed foot** on your sewing machine.

This special foot does not normally come with a sewing machine and must be purchased separately. It is worth the investment. Quilting with the walking foot is easy to do and does not require any special skills. Quilt with a cotton, polyester or metallic thread that matches the color palette of the jacket. Match the bobbin thread to the color of the sweatshirt, so that the quilting stitches blend into the lining. Use the walking foot on your sewing machine to quilt **"in the ditch," next to the lower side of the topstitched seam (the side without the topstitched line of stitching - see photo)**. This stabilizes the Layered Waves fabrics on top of the sweatshirt pieces. The entire jacket can be quilted in flowing lines that complement the curves and angles in the Layered Waves fabrics.

Free-Motion Quilting

If you want to quilt something fancier than flowing lines with the walking foot, try free-motion quilting. If you can write your name with a pen on paper you can do it with a needle and thread on fabric! It simply takes a little practice.

Let the fabric designs suggest the quilting design, either echo the design by adding more of the same pattern in the quilting or simply outline the motifs. Showcase intricate free motion designs on solid fabric.

Here's what you need to do free-motion quilting:

- o   Sewing machine capable of lowering the feed dogs,
- o   75/11 embroidery or quilting needle
- o   Thread to match fabric in top spool and bobbin
- o   Darning foot or free-motion foot

Drop the feed dogs. Look in your sewing machine manual under "darning," "free-motion" or "free-hand quilting" for instructions on how to drop the feed dogs. This disengages the lower mechanism, which moves the fabric, so that YOU are now in control of how, when, and where, the fabric moves!

Practice first on a small "quilt sandwich" (top fabric/batting/ bottom fabric) to be sure the thread tension on your machine is correct. Adjust the top and/or bobbin tension as necessary. Secure beginning and ending stitches with 4-5 small stitches. Here are some exercises to get you started.

1. Warm up with pencil and paper first, by writing your name in script, drawing circles, squares, spirals, zigzag lines, leaves, flowers, absolutely anything…..fill the page with designs. Once you are warmed up, try the same designs on the sewing machine that you drew on paper.

2. Sew fast and then sew slowly. Notice how the speed affects the size of the stitches. Move the practice "quilt sandwich" to the right and left, then up and down. Practice until you feel comfortable. Relaxing music and your favorite drink will help get you "in the flow."

> ### Less is More!
> *Free motion quilting adds beauty and interest to the jacket, but it can also cause pattern pieces to shrink as much as an inch.* **Too much quilting, whether free-motion or with the walking foot, can also flatten the jacket pattern piece and make it stiff and uncomfortable to wear.** *Start with the walking foot quilting to stabilize the pattern pieces then add areas of free motion quilting sparingly.*

Jacket & Vest Assembly

Use a **3/8" seam allowance**, which keeps the sweatshirt as close to the original size after re-construction as possible. Please note that the fabric grain is not an issue at any time during the assembly process. The quilting stitches and the sweatshirt base stabilize the fabrics so they hang beautifully.

After the quilting is finished steam press each pattern piece on the fabric side. This contracts the fabric and gives it an antique crinkled look – this will happen after the first washing too. Trim the edges of the fabric and the sweatshirt so that they are even. Use a rotary cutter and ruler to make sure the ends of the sleeves are straight (not necessary if the curved cuff bands are still attached). Baste an optional neckline facing to the inside of the back pattern piece at this time.

Neckline Facing (optional)
Choose a fun fabric (or leftover scraps from making the Layered Waves fabrics), that you will enjoy seeing every time you put your jacket on.

1. Cut a rectangle, approximately 18"W x 9"L of the facing fabric.
2. Position the back pattern piece (smooth sweatshirt side up) on top of the facing fabric (right side up) and use it as a guide to cut the curve of the neckline and the shoulder edges. Extend the facing as long as you want along the shoulder edges.
3. Remove the back pattern piece from the facing fabric.
4. Cut a half circle (square or triangle) along the bottom portion of the facing fabric. Press the curved edge ¼" toward the wrong side of the fabric.
   *For the **one-piece construction jackets**: press the two edges, that align with the zigzag stitched shoulder seams, ¼" toward the wrong side of the fabric.*
5. Align the raw edges of the neckline facing (right side up) with the raw edges of the back pattern piece (smooth sweatshirt side up). Baste the neckline facing in place with thread.

*For the **"Cheerful" vest,** please go to page 71 to continue assembly instructions.*
*For the **"Playful"** and **"Wild Woman"** jackets (one-piece construction), skip to step #5 on next page*

23

Shoulder & Armhole Seams

1. With right sides together pin the two front pieces to the back piece at the shoulder seams. Sew the two shoulder seams with a 3/8″ seam. A walking foot is helpful for sewing the thick seams. It is also useful for the zigzag stitch.

2. Trim the seams to ¼″ and zigzag or serge with a thread that matches the sweatshirt.

3. Press the shoulder seams toward the back piece.

4. **Pin the sleeves to the corresponding armholes with right sides together (photo at right),** by matching the registration marks. Sew a 3/8″ seam. Clip to ease if necessary. Trim to ¼″ and zigzag stitch or serge with thread that matches the color of the sweatshirt. Press the armhole seam towards the sleeve.

5. Pin-baste the sleeve and side seams (with right sides of the jacket out) and carefully try the jacket on to see if the sleeves are the correct length.

   • **Are the sleeves too long?** Trim them to the length desired + an extra ½″. I prefer having a longer sleeve that can be rolled up.

   • **Are the sleeves too short?** Add a fabric lining that can be rolled up OR cut the sleeves to a point just below the elbow to create three quarter sleeves.

   • **Are the cuffs too tight?** Plan on cuffs that open at the end with a 3″ slit. Refer to page 28 on how to bind the edges or simply open the cuff seam after sewing to create the slit (see two middle photos).

   • **Are the cuffs too wide?** This is easily fixed when the jacket is finished. Pleat the fabrics to the desired width and sew a button through all the layers. Stylish, practical and easy to do! (photo at right)

Too tight after sewn? Use a seam ripper to open the finished cuff ...

... then turn the raw edges in ¼″ toward the inside and hand sew.

Cuff Binding

Before sewing the sleeve and side seams, add the cuff bindings or partial sleeve lining. Allow a minimum of 2″ for a binding and up to 6½″ for a partial sleeve lining that can be rolled up to create a shorter sleeve.

1. Place the sleeve *(fabric side up)* on top of a 2½″ or 6½″ strip (in photo) of cuff binding fabric *(wrong side up)* that is slightly wider than the cuff end of the sleeve. Align one of the long raw edges of the fabric strip with the end of the cuff.

2. Cut along the two sleeve edges to make the pattern piece for the cuff binding.

If the cuff band is still on, cut the bottom edge of the cuff binding fabric to match the curve of the cuff band.

3. Press the edge of the cuff pattern piece that is parallel to the cuff edge, ¼″ toward the wrong side of the fabric.

4. Pin the cuff pattern piece on top of the sleeve *with right sides together.*
   Sew a ¼″ seam at the end of the sleeve only.

5. Press the seam toward the cuff binding fabric so that the cuff pattern piece extends out beyond the sleeve. Repeat these steps for the other cuff.

25

Sleeve and Side Seams

1. Lay the jacket with **right sides together** flat on a table. The cuff binding fabrics should also be extended with right sides together.
2. Align the side seams and match the underarm seams and pin. If the edges to do not align perfectly, trim them carefully with scissors to match.

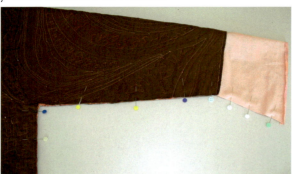

3. Sew a 3/8″ seam from the end of the cuff binding fabric, along the underarm of the sleeve, down the sides to the bottom of the jacket.

4. **Try the jacket on with the wrong sides out.** Check the width of the sleeves.
   - **Are the sleeves too wide?** Take the seam in to adjust. Use a ruler to mark a line that begins at the armhole seam and tapers to the end of the sleeve.

   If the cuff needs to be made tighter also, mark the cuff binding fabric parallel to the edge so that it will match the shape of the sleeve when it is turned back inside. Sew along these marked lines. **Try the jacket on again.** If it fits, cut ¼″ from the new line of stitching. If not, re-stitch the seam till you get the fit you are looking for.

5. Trim the seams to ¼″ and zigzag stitch or serge the edges with thread that matches the color of the sweatshirt.
6. For each sleeve, flip the cuff binding back toward the inside of the jacket. For a hidden cuff binding, press the cuff binding back so that is not visible from edge of the cuff. For a contrasting cuff binding that shows, press the fabric so that 1/8″-¼″ of the cuff binding fabric is visible. Thread-baste the cuff binding.
7. Turn the jacket so that right sides are out. Stitch 1/8″ from the cuff edge of each sleeve with a matching thread.
8. **Try the jacket on again. Is the overall length where you want it?** Is it even? Trim the bottom edge with a rotary cutter and ruler to the desired length.

Bindings

Chose from these two easy bindings to finish your jacket. The **Visible Binding accents the edge** of the jacket with a ¼" band of fabric in either a contrasting or matching fabric. The **Hidden Binding subtly finishes the edges** of the jacket **without becoming part of the jacket design**.

Use leftover fabrics to cut strips either on the bias OR on the straight of the grain. The curve of the neckline in these jackets is very gentle, so that a straight cut binding works just fine. Exceptions are the bolero shrug ("Frisky"), the doll jacket and the teddy bear vest (the "Irresistibles"), which require bias bindings. A bias binding is cut at a 45° angle to the grain line of the fabric and therefore has more "stretch" to go around tight curves.

Visible Binding

1. For a narrow binding cut 2" wide strips x the length needed to go around the edges of the entire jacket (if you want a wider binding, cut 2½" wide strips (see photo Visible Binding).
2. Join the strips together with a straight or 45° angled seam. At one end of the 2" strip, press ¼" under toward the wrong side. This will be your starting point
3. Press the strip in half lengthwise with wrong sides together.
4. Align the raw edges of the strip with the raw edges of the right side of the jacket. Pin in place. As you come to a corner, flip the fabric strip up at a 45° angle. Then fold it down again aligned with the edges of the next side. Continue pinning
5. To finish pinning, insert the tail of the binding into the starting point. Trim the tail to 1" and insert into binding.
6. Machine stitch ¼" from edge. As you come to a corner, flip the fold over and stitch to the crease line (see photo at right).
7. Lift presser foot up (do not cut thread), flip the fold back over, put the presser foot down and begin stitching from the edge of fabric
8. Flip the binding around to the inside of the jacket and hand stitch, so that the line of machine stitching is covered. Miter the corners as you come to them.
9. Hand-stitch the optional neckline facing and the sleeve binding.

Visible Binding

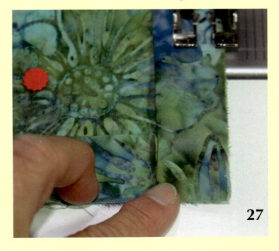

Hidden Binding

1. Cut one **2½″ wide strip x the length** (plus a little extra) needed to go around the edges of the jacket, from the **bottom front corner up and around the neck and down to the other bottom front corner.**
2. Cut another **2½″ wide strip x the length** (plus a little extra) needed for the **bottom edge of the jacket**.

   Open Cuff Hidden Bindings: cut two 2½″ wide strips x the length (plus a little extra) of each opened cuff and four 2½″wide x 4″ long strips.

   Crew Neck: cut two 2½″ wide strips x the length (plus a little extra) of each front pattern piece and cut one 2½″ wide strip x the length (plus a little extra) of the neckline.

   Vest: cut two 2½″ wide strips x the length (plus a little extra) of each armhole.

3. Join the strips together, where necessary, with a straight or 45° angled seam.

Hidden Binding

4. Cut one end of the 2½″ strips with a straight cut (not at a 45° angle). Press this edge ¼″ toward the wrong side. This will be your starting point.
5. Press the strips in half lengthwise with wrong sides together.
6. Align the raw edges of the binding with the raw edges of the jacket (right side up). Pinning is optional. **Start at the bottom front corner by aligning the pressed ¼″ end of the binding** with the bottom edge of the jacket. Machine stitch a ¼″ seam, going up the front, around the neck and down to the other bottom front corner. **Right before you come to the end of stitching the binding strip, stop and trim the strip ¼″ longer than the edge.** Finger press ¼″ toward the wrong side of the strip and align this pressed edge with the edge of the jacket. Continue machine stitching to the edge and secure with a backstitch.

   Crew Neck: This neckline requires two extra steps. Follow the basic instructions described in step #6. First machine stitch the bindings to the two inner front edges and use an iron to press the binding toward the inside of the jacket. Then machine stitch the binding to the neckline edge and press the binding toward the inside of the jacket.

7. Flip the binding around to the inside of the jacket so that it is not visible from the front. Press with an iron.
8. Repeat steps 6-7 for the bottom binding, starting and stopping at the front bottom corners.

   Open Cuff Hidden Binding: Align the two 2½″ x 4″ binding strips on either side of the slit cuff (raw edges together/right sides together). If necessary, remove some of the sleeve seam stitching so that the cuff binding can lie flat along the slit edge. Align the pressed ends of the bindings with the edge of the cuff and machine stitch both with a ¼″ seam and end by turning the end under ¼″ toward the wrong side of the binding. Press both bindings toward the inside of the cuff, so that they are not visible. Attach the binding strip to the edge of the cuff. Repeat for the other cuff.

9. Machine stitch either 1/8″ or ¼″ from all the pressed binding edges of the jacket to secure the Hidden Binding from appearing in the front.
10. Hand-stitch the outer edge of the binding to the inside of the jacket with matching thread. Hand-stitch the optional neckline facing and the cuff binding.
    Re-stitch the sleeve seams if they were opened to stitch the Open Cuff Hidden Binding

Fabric Button Loops

1. Position and sew the button(s) on the jacket.
2. Cut a 1½" wide x 4½" strip (or the length needed to go around the button and back, plus a little extra). For a wider loop, cut a 2" wide strip.
3. Press both long edges of the strip in to the middle toward the wrong side of fabric. Then press in half again.
4. Machine stitch 1/8" from the two pressed edges.

5. Circle the button with the fabric strip to create a snug closure. Extend the ends of the fabric strip across to the other side of the jacket. Trim the ends ¾" from either the line of stitching from the Hidden Binding or ¾" from the edge of a Visible Binding.

6. Remove the fabric strip from the button and reposition it so that it faces the opposite direction. Twist the fabric strip once to create the "loop." Align the ends of the strips 1/8" from the line of stitching or binding edge.

7. Pin and machine stitch the strips 1/8" from the edges.

8. Fold the fabric loop over in the direction of the button, and stitch ¼" from the folded loop. Secure the start and stop stitches with a back-stitch.

Other Button Closure Options

Use a leather cord, seen in this photo on the "Natural" jacket. The ends of the cord are sewn and hidden on the inside of the jacket.

Black ribbons are used as button loops on the "Energetic" jacket (page 39). Other possibilities include yarn, twine, etc….anything that you can "loop"

Soften with a Wash:
If the jacket fits, but feels a little "stiff" - a gentle washing and line drying will relax the fabrics. The washing blends the sweatshirt and the Layered Waves fabrics so that they become "one" and drape easier. You can use the clothes dryer on a low setting as long as the fabrics have been pre-washed. If the fabrics have not been pre-washed, the jacket can shrink as much as 1" on the sleeves and in the overall fit. If in doubt, lay the jacket flat to dry.

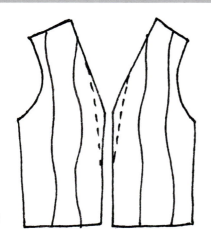

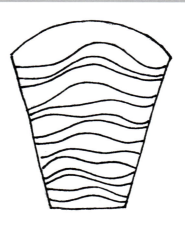

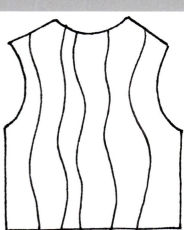

Sporty

Easy gentle curves make this a great beginner jacket. Make it in every-day denim colors with pockets cut from old jeans or dress it up in sophisticated earthy colors. Either way it will be the jacket you grab when you are running out the door!

Fabric Placement Decisions

- All 6 fabrics are used in the front and back of this jacket. Use 3 fabrics on one side and the remaining 3 fabrics on the other side.
- The same fabric order will be used for the back pattern piece.
- The Primary Color/Fabric in this jacket is the denim blue color.

Layered Waves Front

Measure the width of a front pattern piece. Divide that number by 3. Use that number as a guide to cutting the width of the fabric strips to create the Layered Waves fabric that runs in a vertical direction in the front.

Layered Waves Back

Use all 6 fabrics to create a Layered Waves fabric that runs vertically down the back. The width and length of the strips should be the same as the front pattern pieces, but measure again, just to verify.

Use the same sequence of 6 fabrics as was used in the front. The fabric strips are not supposed to align exactly at the shoulder seams, so don't worry about trying to match them.

Sleeves

Begin making a Layered Waves fabric at the wide end of the sleeve, keeping the distance between layers ¼"- 2". Work toward the narrow end, so the waves are oriented to "wrap around" the arm.

Recycle Old Jeans

Cut out the pockets from an old pair of jeans and use it for the front and/or inside pockets on the jacket. Use the belt loops for either hanging loops or button closures. I used the yoke of a favorite jeans shirt as a neckline facing and a belt loop for hanging (see photo page 30).

Continue with "Quilting" on page 21

Optional High V-Cut for Front Pattern Pieces

Measure the distance from the neck-line to the bottom of the sweatshirt. Divide that number by 3 to get the one-third measurement of the jacket front. Mark **one-third down from the top** on the inside edges of both front pattern pieces. Use a rotary cutter and ruler to cut from the one-third mark to the inside corner of the shoulder (where the shoulder edge meets the neckline edge).

Holly's "Sporty" jacket in earthy browns and metallic golds

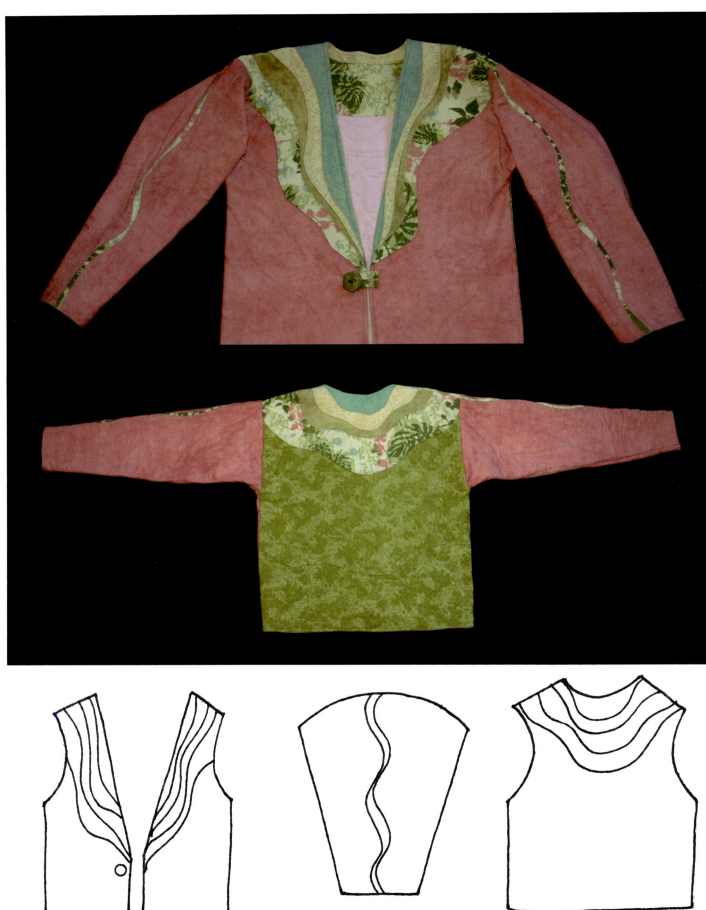

34

Radiant

Imagine yourself in this jacket in your favorite color. Gentle curves hug your neck and shoulders, while delicate ribbon waves accent the sleeves. Feminine, simple and flattering.

Fabric Placement Decisions

- Use the Primary Color/Fabric for the jacket front and sleeves. The Primary Color/Fabric in this jacket is the color pink.
- Decide which fabric will be the ribbon running down the center of the sleeves.
- Select the fabric sequence for the front Layered Waves fabrics. **What color blouse/top do you imagine yourself wearing with this jacket?** Ideally it should contrast with the inner edge of the jacket.
- The order of the Layered Waves fabric for the back yoke is the same as the front. It is not intended to match exactly at the shoulders, but by using the same fabric sequence in the back your eye will still flow over and around.
- Which fabric for the back? It may be whatever yardage you have left. Remember this is a "Creative Topstitching Opportunity."

Front Low V-Cut

Measure the distance from the neckline to the bottom of the sweatshirt. Divide that number by 3 to get the one-third measurement of the jacket front. Mark **one-third up from the bottom** on the inside edges of both front pattern pieces.

Use a rotary cutter and ruler to cut from the one-third mark to the inside corner of the shoulder (where the shoulder edge meets the neckline edge).

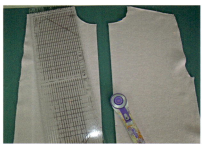

Ribbon Sleeves

1. Lay the sweatshirt sleeve pattern pieces (fuzzy side up) on top of the sleeve fabric (right side up). Cut approximately 1" around the edge of the sweatshirt sleeve pattern pieces.
2. Remove the sweatshirt sleeve pattern piece from the sleeve fabric.
3. Fold the sleeve fabric pattern piece in half and crease it to mark the center of the sleeve. Use this creased line as a guide to cut a gentle curve down the center of the sleeve with a rotary cutter.
4. Press both curved edges ¼" toward the back of the fabric.
5. Place these two curved strips (right side up) on top of the chosen "ribbon" fabric (right side up) Adjust the width of the ribbon to range from ¼"- ½". Pin in place.
6. Before topstitching, place the sweatshirt sleeve pattern piece (fuzzy side down) on top of the pinned fabric (wrong side up) to make sure it still fits. Adjust if necessary by repinning the fabric.
7. Topstitch and cut away the excess fabric on the back. Repeat steps 1-6 for the other sleeve.

Layered Waves Front

1. Measure the distance from the one-third mark (see pencil point in photo) to the outside shoulder corner + 4″.
2. Cut a 4″ wide strip x that measurement, with a gentle curve to begin your Layered Waves fabric.
3. **Mark the "bottom"** of the first fabric in the Layered Waves fabric so you know where it is. **Otherwise you may radiate the strips in the wrong direction.** Make a Layered Waves fabric with the remaining three fabrics that radiates small at the bottom (one-third mark) and gets slightly larger toward the shoulder seam. Press the curved edge of the fourth fabric ¼″ to the wrong side of the fabric.
4. Repeat for the other front pattern piece, using the fabrics in the same sequence.
5. Position both front Layered Waves fabrics (right sides up) on both sweatshirt front pattern pieces (fuzzy sides up), so that the outer edge (the fourth fabric) angles from the one-third mark to the outside shoulder edge. If the fourth fabric extends further than the edge of the shoulder, re-cut the Layered Waves fabric and press it to make it fit. If it is too short, layer and topstitch another piece of the same fabric to make it fit.
6. Carefully lift the outer edge of the Layered Waves fabric up and insert the uncut Primary Color/Fabric underneath. Position it so that it covers the sweatshirt pattern piece below. Slide a small cutting mat between the fabric pattern piece and the sweatshirt pattern piece so that you can pin the two pieces together. **Do not pin to the sweatshirt!** Topstitch and trim. Repeat for the other front piece.

Layered Waves Back

Start making the Layered Waves fabric at the neckine edge. Measure the distance between the points of the inside of the neckline + 4″. Cut a rectangle that measures 4″ x that measurement. From that rectangle cut a half circle with a gently curved line. Add the four remaining fabrics to create a "petal-like" back yoke for the neckline.

Place the back yoke Layered Waves fabric (right sides up) on top of the sweatshirt back pattern piece (fuzzy side up). Carefully lift the outer edge of the Layered Waves fabric up and insert the uncut back fabric. Pin, topstitch and trim.

Continue with "Quilting" on page 21

Energetic

Zig zag waves mixed with gentle curves add extra energy to this classy jacket. Simple one fabric sleeves are made elegant with the addition of gentle lines of Layered Waves at the cuffs.

Fabric Placement Decisions

- Select the Primary Color/Fabric for the sleeves. The Primary Color/Fabric in this jacket is the solid black fabric.
- What order would you like to place the 6 fabrics in the front Layered Waves fabrics? It's nice to start with a specific sequence, but it can and most likely will be changed at any time during the design process.
- Which fabric will form the zigzag wave on the right front panel? Use fabrics that have a high contrast so that the triangles are easy to see.

Sleeve and Layered Waves Cuff Accent

1. Gently iron both sleeves, if necessary. Position the sweatshirt sleeve pattern piece (fuzzy side down) on top of the sleeve fabric (right side down). Smooth gently to remove any wrinkles.
2. Cut the fabric outside the edge of the pattern piece approximately 1", this allows for shrinkage due to quilting.
3. Remove the sweatshirt pattern piece from the newly cut sleeve fabric.
4. Mark the sleeve fabric with chalk 3" above the end of the sleeve.
5. Cut a gentle curve at the 3" mark of the sleeve fabric. Save this 3" piece to end the Layered Waves fabric sequence.
6. Create a Layered Waves fabric with the 5 coordinated fabrics. Start at the end of the sleeve fabric and extend to the end of the cuff. **Space layers ¼" - ¾"** apart. In other words, **very close**. End the Layered Waves fabric with the 3" piece of sleeve fabric. Repeat the above steps for the second sleeve.

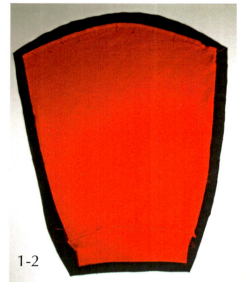

1-2

4

6

40

Layered Waves Front and Back

Use all 6 fabrics to create a Layered Waves fabric that runs vertically on the two front pattern pieces and the back pattern piece. **On one of the front pattern pieces include a zigzag wave.** Be sure to use a contrasting fabric, perhaps one of the solids, so that the zigzag stands out. **Create a corresponding zigzag wave on the back pattern piece.** This does not have to be an exact match at the shoulder seam.

Continue with "Quilting" on page 21

Optional High V-Cut for Front Pattern Pieces

Measure the distance from the neckline to the bottom of the sweatshirt. Divide that number by 3 to get the one-third measurement of the jacket front. Mark **one-third down from the top** on the inside edges of both front pattern pieces. Use a rotary cutter and ruler to cut from the one-third mark to the inside corner of the shoulder (where the shoulder edge meets the neckline edge).

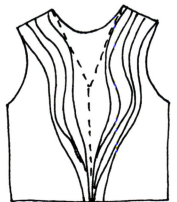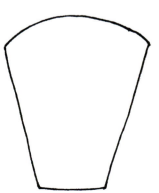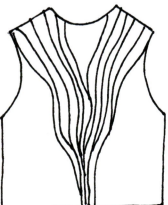

Natural

Flowing lines radiate up and out like the branches of a tree.
Try it in soothing Mother Earth colors or in vibrant floral hues.

Fabric Placement Decisions

- Select the Primary Color/Fabric for the front, back and one of the sleeves. Look for small-scale prints, dark colors and/or parallel line prints placed to run vertically to create a slimming effect.
- The Primary Color/Fabric in this jacket is the green/brown striped fabric.
- The 6 fabrics are used in a random order in the front and back "V" designs.

Front V Cut

Fold the front pattern piece in half lengthwise.

Measure the distance from the neckline to the bottom of the sweatshirt. Divide that number by 3.

Mark the one-third mark from the top of the pattern piece. Use a rotary cutter and ruler to cut from the one-third mark to the inside corner of the shoulder.

Open up the front pattern piece

Layered Waves Front

1. Begin in the center of the front pattern piece by cutting a long triangle with curves on both sides.
2. Press both curved edges of the triangle toward the wrong side of the fabric. **Begin the Layered Waves fabric from the right pressed curved edge of the triangle and work layers at an angle from the center of the bottom edge toward the top right corner of the shoulder.** Keep the distance between the layers very close (½"- 1"). Add slender points (see page 19) to the Layered Waves.
3. Repeat this process working from the left side of the triangle toward the top left corner of the shoulder.
4. Add the Primary Color/Fabric on both sides of the Layered Waves to cover the sweatshirt front pattern piece. Trim the center triangle fabric ½" larger than the sweatshirt pattern piece.
5. Cut a gently curved line (or a straight line) down the center of the Layered Waves front fabric to create the two front panels.

44

Layered Waves Back

1. Begin with the "V" shape fabric cut away from the center triangle used in creating the Layered Waves front pattern piece. If you don't have this piece or can't find it, cut a small triangle from the same fabric used in the front center triangle.

2. Start making waves working from the center triangle toward the left direction. Cut a curve on the first fabric. Press the curved edge toward the wrong side and topstitch it to the triangle.

3. Create a "Crest" (see page 17 for definition) by cutting a curve on the other side of this first fabric. Press this curve and continue making waves that angle from the bottom center of the pattern piece up toward the top corner of the left shoulder.

4. Once the left side of the Layered Waves is complete, do the same for the right side by starting with the right side of the small triangle. Press the right edge of the triangle + the previous fabric from the left side of the Layered Waves fabric.

5. Continue making waves that angle from the center bottom to the top corner of the right shoulder.

6. Add the Primary Color/Fabric on both sides of the Layered Waves to cover the sweatshirt back pattern piece. Pin, topstitch and trim.

Sleeves

Use one piece of fabric to cover each of the sleeve pattern pieces. Both sleeves can be made with the same fabric or use different fabrics like I did!

I used Creative Topstitching with my leftover fabrics to create sleeves that have additional textural interest and curved designs.

Continue with "Quilting" on page 21

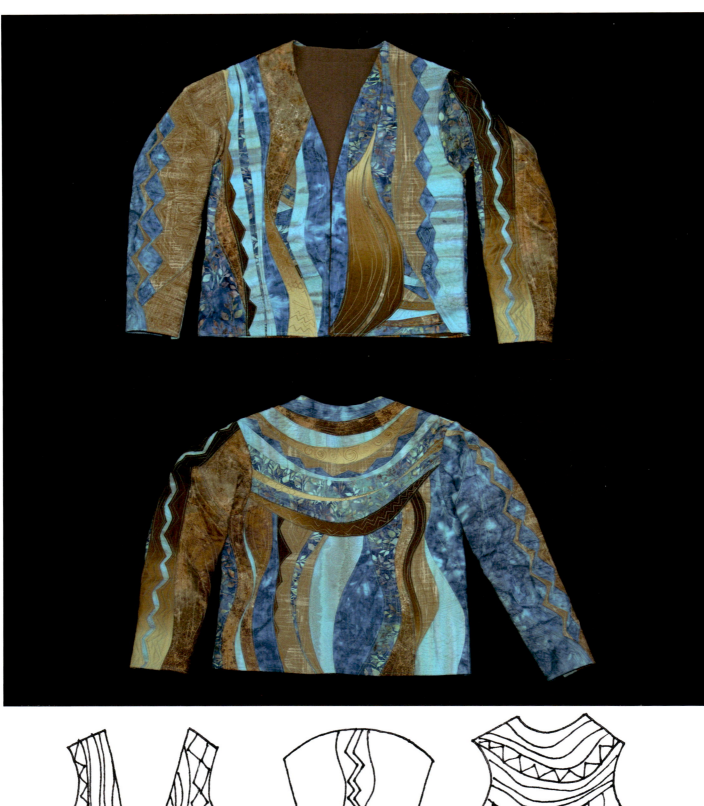

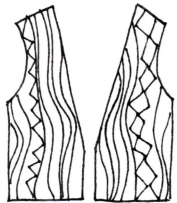

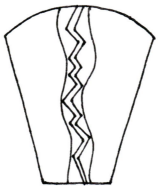

Spontaneous

Are you ready to cut loose and play? This is a "design as you go" jacket. Combine wild waves, zig zag waves, lightning streak and jaunty hanging diamond waves in the colors of your choice and at your whim!

Fabric Placement Decisions

- The Primary Fabric in this jacket is the blue leaf print fabric.
- The Primary Color is blue/turquoise
- Decide on the fabrics for the sleeve lightning streak and/or jaunty hanging diamond waves

Layered Waves Yoke and Back

1. **Begin with a 1/2 yard of fabric cut approximately 4″ wider than the width of the back pattern piece.**

   Cut a swooping "U" curve to begin creating the Layered Waves fabric for the back yoke.

2. Measure the maximum distance from the bottom of the yoke to the bottom of the sweatshirt pattern piece. Make a vertical Layered Waves fabric to fill the space below the yoke. Vertical lines provide a "slimming" effect to balance the horizontal yoke lines.

3. Pin and topstitch the horizontal Layered Waves yoke section to the vertical Layered Waves fabric.

Lightning Streak Sleeves

Choose a ribbon, lightning streak or jaunty hanging diamonds wave to run down the length of the sleeve. Try a different type for each sleeve.

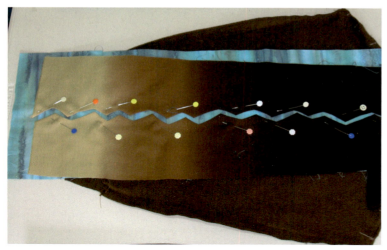

Place the lightning streak down the center of the sleeve pattern piece. Use Creative Topstitching to fill in the fabrics to cover the sweatshirt pattern piece.

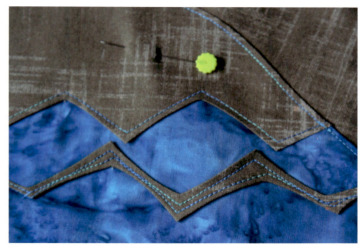

This design is a combination of a jaunty hanging diamond and a variation of the Lightning Streak. By cutting a zigzag that matches the edge of the diamond, a "crest" is formed. Notice that there is topstitching on both edges of the fabric.

Layered Waves Front

Use the remaining fabrics to create vertical Layered Waves fabrics for each of the front pattern pieces. Base your decisions on the fabrics chosen for the sleeves.

Continue with "Quilting" on page 21

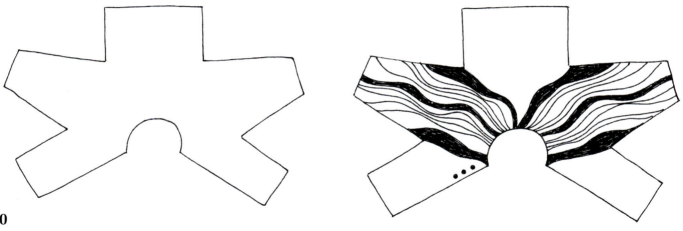

Playful

Feel relaxed and casual in this one-piece construction jacket.
Waves flow smoothly from the neckline to the end of the sleeve, because the sweatshirt seams have been taken apart and basted together so that they lay flat (see page 13).

Fabric Placement Decisions

- Do you want the same fabric on both front pattern pieces or different fabrics?
- The back pattern piece needs yardage. Select from your Primary Color/Fabric or use Creative Topstitching to make the size needed to fit.
- The Primary Color/Fabric in this jacket is the color blue/green.
- Select a dark solid-like fabric for the Center Wave going down the middle of each sleeve and the diagonal wave, which runs from the neckline to the underarm.

Layered Waves Sleeves

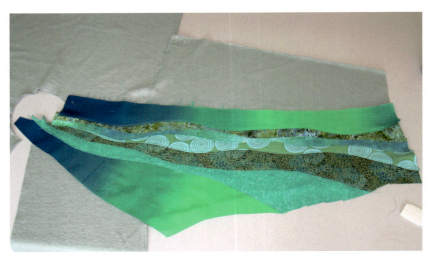

1. **Begin with a 3″ wide strip of the Center Wave fabric x the length of the center of the sleeve + 2″.**

   Cut a curve on one side of the strip, press the edge under to the wrong side and make waves with the remaining 5 fabrics that are very close together at the neckline and get wider toward edge of the sleeve.

   End with the Center Wave fabric you began with. Cut this diagonal wave so that it runs from the corner point of the neckline to the underarm (where the sleeve and side edges meet).

2. Repeat this process to make waves with the 5 fabrics for the back side of the sleeve.

Stay Centered:
Each time you reposition the Layered Waves fabric on the sweatshirt sleeve pattern, be sure to align the center wave with the center of the neckline and the middle of the sleeve.

Fanning the Waves:
As you add each new fabric, position it on top of the sweatshirt pattern piece to determine how to cut it. Mark the cutting line with chalk and cut with scissors. This is the easiest way to make sure the angle is correct and that you have enough fabric to cover the sleeve.

Add the Front & Back Fabrics
This is the only jacket style in the book where part of the Layered Waves fabric is sewn directly to the sweatshirt pattern piece.

1. Press the curved edges under on the last diagonal wave fabrics on the front and back Layered Waves fabrics. This last curve should not be too curvy, more like a line so that it isn't too distracting.
2. Place the Layered Waves sleeve fabrics (right sides up) on top of the sweatshirt pattern piece (fuzzy side up)
3. Position and slide the fabric for the front pattern piece under the last diagonal fabric. Mark with chalk where the fabric will tuck under the last diagonal fabric (you can feel this with your fingers) Trim ¼" away from the chalk line, so that this ¼" will tuck under the diagonal wave.
4. Pin the pressed diagonal wave to the front panel fabric and **topstitch to the sweatshirt.**
5. Repeat for the other front panel and the back.

Thread Baste! NOTE
Although pin basting is quick, this jacket style needs to be folded and "scrunched" often in order to quilt. These actions cause the pins to stick out, causing painful pricks. Take the time to thread baste the entire sweatshirt before quilting. Another basting option is to use basting safety pins.

Continue with "Quilting" on page 21

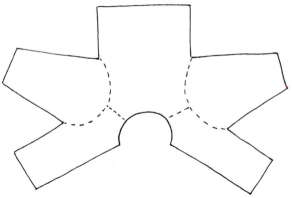

Wild Woman

This one-piece construction jacket calls out to your adventurous spirit. Waves flow smoothly around the neck and shoulder, because the sweatshirt seams have been taken apart and basted together so that they lay flat (see page 13).

CAUTION! This jacket is not for the feint of heart!

There aren't any specific directions to follow, just guidelines for you to pursue your creative intuition. Are you willing to cut into your fabrics with wild abandon and design as-you-go? Do you have a sense of adventure and the ability to enjoy the journey, not quite knowing what the final destination is?
If this sounds like you, then you are ready for the Wild Woman jacket!

Making "Wavelengths"

Wavelengths are Layered Waves fabrics that begin with a fat quarter (18" x 22") instead of a fabric strip measured to fit a pattern piece. We follow the same Layered Waves process of cutting and top-stitching, but because we start with a larger piece of fabric, **the curves (and angles) are larger and wilder.** Also, since we are not making the wavelength to fit the pattern piece, both edges are cut with a curved edge instead of being trimmed straight.

For more projects using "wavelengths" see pages 66 - 91 of the "Layered Waves" book.

A fat quarter is the standard size fabric with which to begin, regardless of whether you are making a size S or a 3XL jacket.

Cut 2 fat quarters (18" x 22") from each of the six fabrics (one half yard yields two fat quarters). You now have 2 sets of fat quarters from each of the six fabrics. Use one set of fat quarters (set = one fat quarter from each of the six fabrics) to make the first wavelength and place the other set of fat quarters aside.

1. **Cut:** Begin making a wavelength by cutting a swooping curve from corner to corner on the fat quarter. Shapes like a giant "S" or "C" make great wavelengths.
   Choose one of the two cut curved shapes (it doesn't matter which one). Set the other cut curved shape aside to be used later.
2. **Press:** Press the curved edge under approximately ¼" to the wrong side of the fabric
3. **Cut again:** Place this fabric with the pressed curved edge on top of a second fabric (right sides up). Cut a curve on the second fabric that is similar to the first curve, varying the distance from the first curve anywhere from ½"- 3".
4. **Pin**.
5. **Topstitch 1/8"** from the pressed edge.
6. **Trim:** Turn the fabric over. Carefully cut the excess fabric from the back away, approximately ¼" from line of topstitching. Save this cut away fabric to use in other wavelengths.

Repeat the above steps with zigzag waves, ribbons, crests, slender points, lightning streaks and jaunty hanging diamond waves (see pages 16-19) to create a wavelength that uses each fabric twice. **A total of 12 fabrics in each wavelength** is suggested. Wavelengths in different sizes work also (see photo on page 57).

Make Three Wavelengths

- Use the first set of fat quarters to make the first wavelength.
- Use the second set of fat quarters to create the second wavelength.
- Use the leftover curved fabric shapes that were cut away from the first and second wavelengths to create a third wavelength. Once the 3 wavelengths are complete, press the curved edges on both sides toward the wrong side of the fabric.

Crewneck or "V" ?

Before the design process begins, decide whether you want to keep the crew neck curve or have a "V" cut. First measure the length of the front panel and divide that number by three. This number will equal one-third of the length of the jacket front.

High "V": Mark a point **one-third down from the top edge** of both front pattern pieces. Use a rotary cutter and ruler to cut from this one-third mark up to the inside corner of the shoulder

Low "V": Mark a point **one-third up from the bottom** edge of both front pattern pieces. Use a rotary cutter and ruler to cut from this one-third mark up to the inside corner of the shoulder

3 Wavelengths
Press the curved edge on *both sides* of the wavelengths, approximately ¼" to the wrong side of the fabric.

Design Process

This next step requires a very large flat surface (not a vertical design wall), such as a large table, 2 tables pushed together, or the floor. See photos below of two different jackets in progress on the floor.

Now it's PLAYTIME! Arrange and re-arrange the wavelengths to wrap around the neck and shoulder areas. The ends of the wavelengths should either extend to the edge of the sweatshirt pattern piece or be tucked under another wavelength. As you audition the different wavelengths in different positions, take digital photographs so that when you do find the perfect layout you can re-create it.

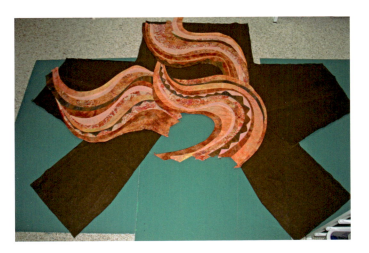

Once you are happy with the placement of the 3 wavelengths, pin them together where they connect. **Do not pin the wavelength to the sweatshirt pattern piece.** Slide a small cutting mat beneath the wavelengths and the sweatshirt to make pinning easier. Topstitch the pinned areas and trim any excess fabric from underneath away.

Carefully lay the topstitched wavelengths back on top of the sweatshirt pattern. Smooth gently to remove any wrinkles in the fabric and the sweatshirt.

Fill in the negative space (the areas where the sweatshirt pattern is showing through) with the remaining larger pieces of fabrics (see photos below). Pin the wavelengths to the fabrics. **Topstitch together, but do not topstitch to the sweatshirt.** Do one or two sections at a time. Use Creative Topstitching to make fabrics fit the pattern pieces.

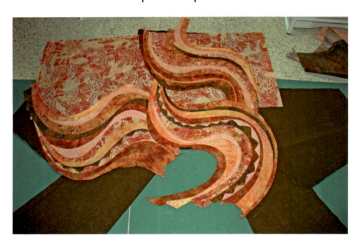 

Continue the Flow *of a wavelength across the front of the jacket (or wherever needed), by re-creating another wavelength in the same fabrics (see the three photos below for the process).*

 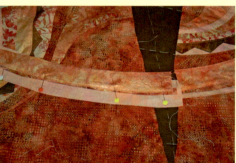 

Thread Baste! NOTE

Although pin basting is quick, this jacket style needs to be folded and "scrunched" often in order to quilt. These actions cause the pins to stick out, causing painful pricks. Take the time to thread baste the entire sweatshirt before quilting. Another basting option is to use basting safety pins.

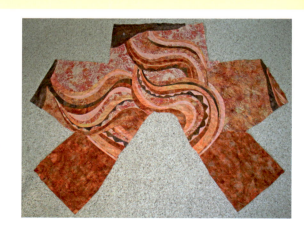

Continue with "Quilting" on page 21

58

Here is the Wild Woman jacket in different colors.
Which colors make you wildly happy?

Vests & Shrugs

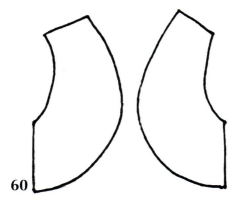

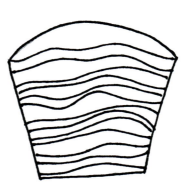

60

Frisky

Bolero Shrug with 3/4 Sleeves

This versatile little jacket will make you feel at home wherever you travel. It's so light and comfortable, you'll forget you have it on.

Fabric Placement Decisions

- Choose your Primary Color/Fabric to feature on the front and the back. The Primary Color/Fabric in this jacket is the small-scale tan print fabric.
- The remaining five fabrics will be layered on the sleeves.

Cutting the Sweatshirt for a Bolero Shrug

1. Put the sweatshirt on. Touch the last bone of your rib cage. Mark it with chalk on both sides of the front of the sweatshirt.

2. On both sleeves, mark approximately 4" below the elbow.
   Lay the sweatshirt (smooth side out) flat on a table. Smooth out the wrinkles. Use a ruler and chalk (or marking pencil) to measure and draw straight lines where indicated by the chalk marks on the bottom edge and sleeves of the sweatshirt.

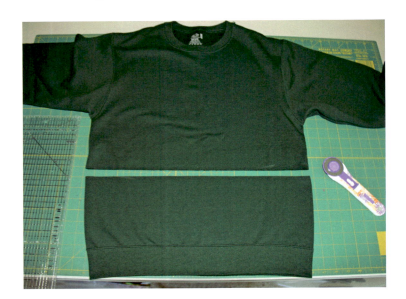

3. Use a rotary cutter and ruler to trim on the marked lines.
   Save the cut away sweatshirt material to make an adorable doll jacket or teddy bear vest. They are simply irresistible! See pages 72-79 for complete instructions.
4. Continue with the cutting instructions at step #2 on page 11.

Front Bolero Cut

1. Measure the width of a front sweatshirt pattern piece. Divide that number by three. Use this number to mark the bottom edge one-third in from the side seam.

2. Use a large round serving plate to help mark a curve on one front pattern piece that ends one-third from the side. Align the plate edge so that it extends from a point on the **INNER NECKLINE EDGE** (**NOT on the shoulder edge**) and flows around to the bottom one-third mark. Use scissors to cut along the marked edge.

   Use the cut front pattern piece as a template for marking and cutting the other front pattern piece.

3. Place both front sweatshirt pattern pieces and the back sweatshirt pattern piece (fuzzy side down) on top of the Primary Color/Fabric (right side down). Smooth any wrinkles.
4. Cut approximately ½" around all of the sweatshirt pattern piece edges.
5. Turn the three units (two front sweatshirt/fabric pieces + one back sweatshirt/fabric piece) over so the right side of the fabric is up. Pin.

Layered Waves Sleeves

Begin making a Layered Waves fabric at the wide end of the sleeve, keeping the distance between layers ¼"- 2". Start at the shoulder and work toward the narrow end of the sleeve, so that the waves are oriented to "wrap around" the arm.

Continue with "Quilting" on page 21

This bolero shrug is cut at the waist instead of just below the rib cage. Very comfortable and versatile.

The back of the shrug features a turtle print fabric (see photo above right)

To **adjust the fit of the bolero shrug,** create a back tuck by pleating the fabrics. Connect with an elastic band (painted brown to match the fabric) and contrasting buttons.

The back of the formal shrug at right is fitted the same way, using a thin black elastic combined with two beads.

Dress up the everyday shrug with fancy fabrics, such as gold lamé, silks, satins, velvets and cottons with metallic gold or silver patterns.

Embellish with beads to add even more sparkle.

I wore this shrug to the formal 57th annual Viennese Opera Ball held at the Waldorf Astoria in New York City. No one guessed that I was wearing a sweatshirt!

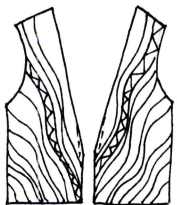

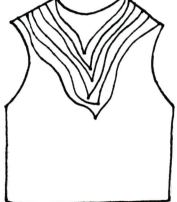

Cheerful
Vest

Here's a perky combination of curves and angles sure to make you smile. For more vest styles, select one of the jacket designs and simply leave off the sleeves!

Fabric Placement Decision

Chose a Primary Color/Fabric for the "faux" lapels, the back and the binding. In this vest the Primary Color/Fabric is the blue fabric with the subtle circle print.

Cutting the Sweatshirt for a Vest

1. Remove the bottom band by cutting just above the stitching line with scissors.
2. **Now try the sweatshirt on**. Decide how long you want the vest to be: hip, mid-hip or waist length. Mark that length with chalk.
3. Lay the sweatshirt flat on a table. Use a ruler to draw a straight line where the chalk mark indicates. Use a ruler and rotary cutter to cut along that line.
4. Press the side seams flat with your fingers. Use scissors to cut open both sides or if there is a seam, undo it with a seam ripper.
5. Continue cutting with scissors just inside of the armhole seam up and over the shoulder to remove the sleeve (see photo at right).

   (PLEASE NOTE that for all jackets in this book, the seams are taken apart with the seam ripper to maintain the original fit of the sweatshirt, but for the vest it is not as critical that the seams stay true to size).

   Repeat to cut the other side and remove the sleeve.
6. Use a seam ripper to undo the shoulder and collar band seams.
7. Fold the sweatshirt front in half and crease to mark the center. Cut up the center with scissors or a rotary cutter to create the two front pattern pieces.
8. Measure the distance from the neckline to the bottom of the sweatshirt. Divide that number by 3 to find the approximate one-third measurement. Mark one-third up from the bottom edge. Use a ruler and rotary cutter to cut from the one-third mark to the inside edge of the shoulder, where the neckline edge meets the shoulder edge.

Save the Sleeves
to make an adorable doll jacket or teddy bear vest. They are simply irresistible! See pages 72-79 for complete instructions.

68

Layered Waves Front

Start with two 4"- 5" wide strips of the Primary Color/Fabric to create the faux lapels. If you want the same curve for both faux lapels, use the reversed curve cut on the first strip as a guide to cut the second curve.

Make a Layered Waves fabric for each front pattern piece that begins with the lapel fabric, and angles to the lower corner.

> **Remember to Adjust Length:**
> *Be careful, as you angle the strips to create the Layered Waves fabric, the length of each strip will need to be different to fit the front pattern piece.*

Layered Triangles Yoke and Back

1. Start with a free form cut triangle of the Primary Color/Fabric.

2. Press the two bottom edges to the wrong side of the fabric.

3. Place this triangle on top of another fabric, right sides facing up, and cut a triangle that is approximately 1" larger than the two bottom edges of the first triangle.

   Cut the top edge even with the top raw edge of the original triangle.

4. Pin in place and topstitch the two bottom pressed edges.

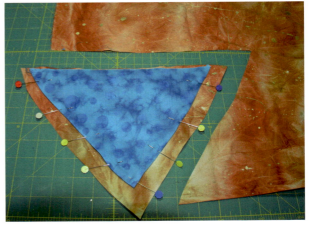

5. Turn over and cut away the back fabric triangle.

6. Repeat this triangle layering process with the remaining 4 fabrics.

7. Place the back sweatshirt pattern piece (fuzzy side down) on top of the Primary Color/Fabric fabric (right side down)

8. Trim ½"-1" around the pattern piece edges

9. Carefully turn the sweatshirt pattern piece/ back fabric over so that the back fabric is right side up. Smooth any wrinkles.

10. Center the Layered Triangles Yoke (right side up) on top of the back fabric (right side up) and **carefully pin the Triangle Yoke to the back fabric**, but NOT through to the sweatshirt pattern piece! (see photo right)

Insert a small cutting mat between the 2 layers to make pinning easier.

11. Remove the pinned Triangle Yoke and back fabric from the sweatshirt pattern piece and topstitch the two bottom edges of the last triangle to the back fabric. Trim the excess fabric from the back.

Use the Leftover Triangles
cut from the Layered Triangle Yoke for an optional neckline facing or fun pockets

Continue with "Quilting" on page 21

Vest Assembly
1. Sew the shoulder seams with a 3/8″ seam. Trim to ¼″ and zigzag stitch the edges.
2. Press the two shoulder seams toward the back pattern piece.
3. Lay the vest down right sides together on a flat surface. Make sure that the front and back armholes match. If not trim them so that they do.
4. Pin the side seams along an imaginary seam line and try the vest on for size
   Are the armholes large enough? In most cases they will not be large enough. Cut them to a comfortable size.

Where does the shoulder seam end? If it is beyond your shoulder, cut it to fit your shoulder.

How do the sides fit? If too wide, pin a new seam until it fits.

5. Sew the side seams and trim the bottom edge with a ruler and rotary cutter.

Continue with "Bindings" on page 27

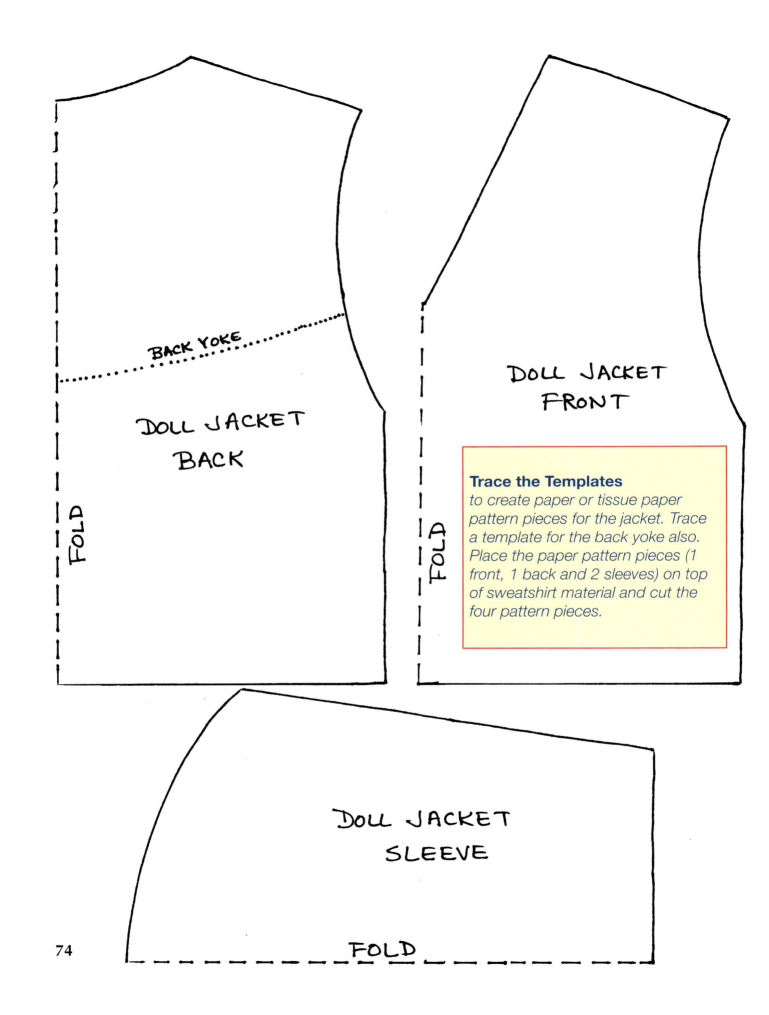

BACK YOKE

DOLL JACKET
BACK

FOLD

DOLL JACKET
FRONT

FOLD

Trace the Templates
to create paper or tissue paper pattern pieces for the jacket. Trace a template for the back yoke also. Place the paper pattern pieces (1 front, 1 back and 2 sleeves) on top of sweatshirt material and cut the four pattern pieces.

DOLL JACKET
SLEEVE

74

FOLD

18" Doll Jacket

Make a little girl very happy with this Wearable Waves jacket for her favorite doll. Perhaps you will want to make a jacket for her that matches the doll's jacket? Simply follow the Doll Jacket instructions, but use the appropriate children's size sweatshirt for the pattern pieces, as we did for the adult size jackets.

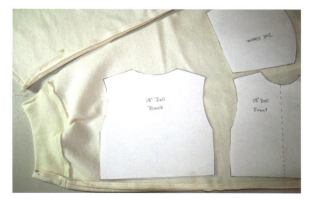

Polyester felt or fleece can be substituted for the sweatshirt material.

Layered Waves Front

Use four fabrics to create a Layered Waves fabric that runs horizontally to fit the front sweatshirt pattern piece (1/4 yard of Primary Color/Fabric + 1/8 yard each of 3 coordinating fabrics) The Primary Color/Fabric in this jacket is the red fabric with the tiny white dots.

Layered Waves Back

1. Choose two fabrics to create the back yoke and bottom section.
2. Place the back yoke template on top of a fabric and cut ½" around all of the edges. Press the bottom curved edge ¼" toward the wrong side of the fabric.
3. Cut the fabric for the bottom section approximately ½" larger than the back pattern piece. **Topstitch the yoke and bottom section together (not to the back pattern piece).** Turn over and trim the excess fabric from the back.
4. Pin the back yoke/bottom section to the back pattern piece.

Sleeves

Cut the Primary Color/Fabric to fit both of the sleeve pattern pieces.

Quilting and assembly is basically the same for the adult jacket, except:

- Sew with ¼" seams.
- Wait until the front Layered Waves fabric is quilted to the sweatshirt pattern piece to cut down the center to create the two front pattern pieces.
- Cuff Binding Shortcut: fold the end of the cuff (fabric and pattern piece) under ¼" toward the wrong side and stitch with a straight stitch or a zigzag stitch.

Teddy Bear Vest

Little boys will be thrilled to dress up their favorite teddy bear or stuffed animal with this cute little vest. This pattern fits a chubby 18"- 21" tall teddy bear. The pattern may need to be adapted to fit the

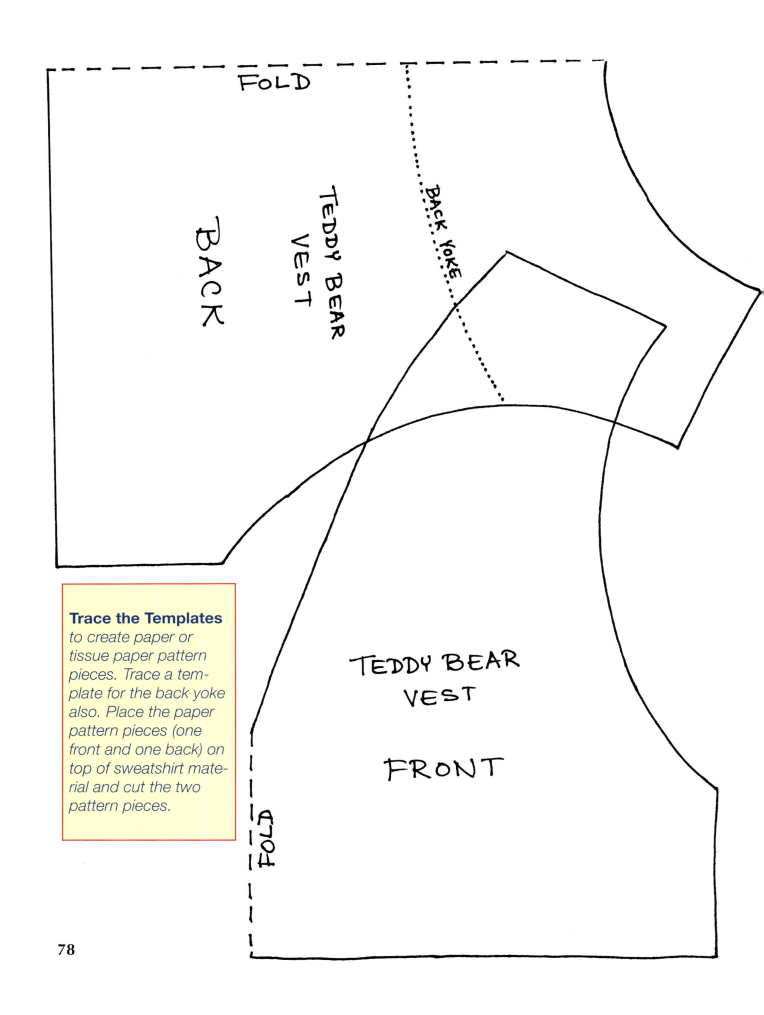

FOLD

TEDDY BEAR
VEST

BACK

BACK YOKE

Trace the Templates
to create paper or tissue paper pattern pieces. Trace a template for the back yoke also. Place the paper pattern pieces (one front and one back) on top of sweatshirt material and cut the two pattern pieces.

TEDDY BEAR
VEST

FRONT

FOLD

Layered Waves Front

Choose a multi-color fabric (1/4 yard) and up to seven coordinating fabrics (1/8 yard of each) to create a Layered Waves fabric that runs horizontally to fit the front sweatshirt pattern piece. The Primary Color/Fabric in this vest is the multi-color print.

Polyester felt or fleece can be substituted for the sweatshirt material.

Layered Waves Back

1. Use the multi-color fabric (Primary Color/Fabric) for the back yoke and one other fabric for the bottom section.
2. Place the back yoke template on top of the multi-color fabric and cut ½″ around all of the edges. Press the bottom curved edge ¼″ toward the wrong side of the fabric.
3. Cut the fabric for the bottom section approximately ½″ larger than the back pattern piece. **Topstitch the yoke and bottom section together (not to the back pattern piece).** Turn over and trim the excess fabric from the back.
4. Pin the back yoke/bottom section to the back pattern piece.

Quilting and assembly is basically the same for the adult vest, except:

• Sew with ¼″ seams.
• Wait until the front Layered Waves fabric is quilted to the sweatshirt pattern piece to cut down the center to create the two front pattern pieces.

Check out Karen's other books ...

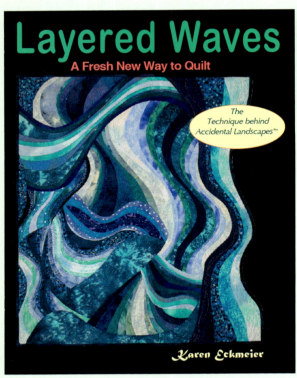

This is the book that inspired Accidental Landscapes and Wearables Waves.

Let your creativity flow as you explore Karen's layered topstitching technique to add graceful curves and dramatic angles to all your fiber art projects: Traditional and contemporary quilts, wearables, hand bags, and so much more!

$24.95 (96 pages full color)

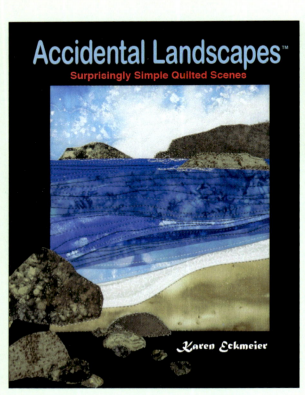

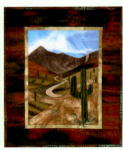

Here is the other "offspring" of Layered Waves. Discover the secrets of creating a fabric landscape "accidentally," using Karen's layered topstitching technique.

Create a landscape in a day! You'll surprise yourself with the lively, exciting compositions. So impressive, and yet so quick!

$21.95 (64 pages full color)